GW00457236

HOUSE
PLANT
CARE LOG

Jayme | Books
DESIGN

A BIG THANK YOU FOR SUPPORTING INDEPENDANT PUBLISHING
WE HOPE YOU ARE HAPPY WITH YOUR PURCHASE

Why not Subscribe to our once a month newsletter
We promise it to be spam free and contain only fun and informative
news and updates on all our latest release and Editor monthly
recommendations.

SIMPLY SCAN THE QR CODE BELOW

REVIEWS ARE IMPORTANT! ★ ★ ★ ★ ★

Your feedback and comments are greatly appreciated
on Facebook and Amazon. Both help us bring the best to you
and our customers. A few seconds of your time would mean
a huge difference to helping us maintain quality standards
Thank you

WHY NOT FIND, FOLLOW AND LIKE US ON FACEBOOK!
Comments, question and reviews are always welcome

HOUSE PLANT *CARE LOG*

Date: / / /

PORCH PLANTS

KITCHENPLANTS

LIVING ROOM PLANTS

SPECIAL PLANTS

#	PLANTS	TYPE	LOCATION	WATERING FREQUENCY
1				
2				
3				
4				
5				
6				
7				
8				
9				
10				
11				

HOUSE PLANT *CARE LOG*

Date: / / /

PORCH PLANTS

KITCHENPLANTS

LIVING ROOM PLANTS

SPECIAL PLANTS

#	PLANTS	TYPE	LOCATION	WATERING FREQUENCY
1				
2				
3				
4				
5				
6				
7				
8				
9				
10				
11				

HOUSE PLANT *CARE LOG*

Date: / / /

PORCH PLANTS

KITCHENPLANTS

LIVING ROOM PLANTS

SPECIAL PLANTS

#	PLANTS	TYPE	LOCATION	WATERING FREQUENCY
1				
2				
3				
4				
5				
6				
7				
8				
9				
10				
11				

HOUSE PLANT *CARE LOG*   *Date: / / /*

PORCH PLANTS

KITCHENPLANTS

LIVING ROOM PLANTS

SPECIAL PLANTS

#	PLANTS	TYPE	LOCATION	WATERING FREQUENCY
1				
2				
3				
4				
5				
6				
7				
8				
9				
10				
11				

HOUSE PLANT *CARE LOG*

Date: / / /

PORCH PLANTS

KITCHENPLANTS

LIVING ROOM PLANTS

SPECIAL PLANTS

#	PLANTS	TYPE	LOCATION	WATERING FREQUENCY
1				
2				
3				
4				
5				
6				
7				
8				
9				
10				
11				

HOUSE PLANT *CARE LOG*

Date: / / /

PORCH PLANTS

KITCHENPLANTS

LIVING ROOM PLANTS

SPECIAL PLANTS

#	PLANTS	TYPE	LOCATION	WATERING FREQUENCY
1				
2				
3				
4				
5				
6				
7				
8				
9				
10				
11				

HOUSE PLANT *CARE LOG*

Date: / / /

PORCH PLANTS

KITCHENPLANTS

LIVING ROOM PLANTS

SPECIAL PLANTS

#	PLANTS	TYPE	LOCATION	WATERING FREQUENCY
1				
2				
3				
4				
5				
6				
7				
8				
9				
10				
11				

HOUSE PLANT *CARE LOG*

Date: / / /

PORCH PLANTS

KITCHENPLANTS

LIVING ROOM PLANTS

SPECIAL PLANTS

#	PLANTS	TYPE	LOCATION	WATERING FREQUENCY
1				
2				
3				
4				
5				
6				
7				
8				
9				
10				
11				

HOUSE PLANT *CARE LOG*

Date: / / /

PORCH PLANTS

KITCHENPLANTS

LIVING ROOM PLANTS

SPECIAL PLANTS

#	PLANTS	TYPE	LOCATION	WATERING FREQUENCY
1				
2				
3				
4				
5				
6				
7				
8				
9				
10				
11				

HOUSE PLANT *CARE LOG*

PORCH PLANTS

KITCHENPLANTS

LIVING ROOM PLANTS

SPECIAL PLANTS

#	PLANTS	TYPE	LOCATION	WATERING FREQUENCY
1				
2				
3				
4				
5				
6				
7				
8				
9				
10				
11				

HOUSE PLANT *CARE LOG*   *Date: / / /*

PORCH PLANTS

KITCHENPLANTS

LIVING ROOM PLANTS

SPECIAL PLANTS

#	PLANTS	TYPE	LOCATION	WATERING FREQUENCY
1				
2				
3				
4				
5				
6				
7				
8				
9				
10				
11				

HOUSE PLANT *CARE LOG*   *Date: / / /*

PORCH PLANTS

KITCHENPLANTS

LIVING ROOM PLANTS

SPECIAL PLANTS

#	PLANTS	TYPE	LOCATION	WATERING FREQUENCY
1				
2				
3				
4				
5				
6				
7				
8				
9				
10				
11				

HOUSE PLANT *CARE LOG*

Date: / / /

PORCH PLANTS

KITCHENPLANTS

LIVING ROOM PLANTS

SPECIAL PLANTS

#	PLANTS	TYPE	LOCATION	WATERING FREQUENCY
1				
2				
3				
4				
5				
6				
7				
8				
9				
10				
11				

HOUSE PLANT *CARE LOG*

Date: / / /

PORCH PLANTS

KITCHENPLANTS

LIVING ROOM PLANTS

SPECIAL PLANTS

#	PLANTS	TYPE	LOCATION	WATERING FREQUENCY
1				
2				
3				
4				
5				
6				
7				
8				
9				
10				
11				

HOUSE PLANT *CARE LOG*

Date: / / /

PORCH PLANTS

KITCHENPLANTS

LIVING ROOM PLANTS

SPECIAL PLANTS

#	PLANTS	TYPE	LOCATION	WATERING FREQUENCY
1				
2				
3				
4				
5				
6				
7				
8				
9				
10				
11				

HOUSE PLANT *CARE LOG*

Date: / / /

PORCH PLANTS

KITCHENPLANTS

LIVING ROOM PLANTS

SPECIAL PLANTS

#	PLANTS	TYPE	LOCATION	WATERING FREQUENCY
1				
2				
3				
4				
5				
6				
7				
8				
9				
10				
11				

HOUSE PLANT *CARE LOG*   *Date: / / /*

PORCH PLANTS

KITCHENPLANTS

LIVING ROOM PLANTS

SPECIAL PLANTS

#	PLANTS	TYPE	LOCATION	WATERING FREQUENCY
1				
2				
3				
4				
5				
6				
7				
8				
9				
10				
11				

HOUSE PLANT *CARE LOG*

Date: / / /

PORCH PLANTS

KITCHENPLANTS

LIVING ROOM PLANTS

SPECIAL PLANTS

#	PLANTS	TYPE	LOCATION	WATERING FREQUENCY
1				
2				
3				
4				
5				
6				
7				
8				
9				
10				
11				

HOUSE PLANT *CARE LOG*   *Date: / / /*

PORCH PLANTS

KITCHENPLANTS

LIVING ROOM PLANTS

SPECIAL PLANTS

#	PLANTS	TYPE	LOCATION	WATERING FREQUENCY
1				
2				
3				
4				
5				
6				
7				
8				
9				
10				
11				

HOUSE PLANT *CARE LOG*

Date: / / /

PORCH PLANTS

KITCHENPLANTS

LIVING ROOM PLANTS

SPECIAL PLANTS

#	PLANTS	TYPE	LOCATION	WATERING FREQUENCY
1				
2				
3				
4				
5				
6				
7				
8				
9				
10				
11				

HOUSE PLANT *CARE LOG*

Date: / / /

PORCH PLANTS

KITCHENPLANTS

LIVING ROOM PLANTS

SPECIAL PLANTS

#	PLANTS	TYPE	LOCATION	WATERING FREQUENCY
1				
2				
3				
4				
5				
6				
7				
8				
9				
10				
11				

HOUSE PLANT *CARE LOG*

Date: / / /

PORCH PLANTS

KITCHENPLANTS

LIVING ROOM PLANTS

SPECIAL PLANTS

#	PLANTS	TYPE	LOCATION	WATERING FREQUENCY
1				
2				
3				
4				
5				
6				
7				
8				
9				
10				
11				

HOUSE PLANT *CARE LOG*

Date: / / /

PORCH PLANTS

KITCHENPLANTS

LIVING ROOM PLANTS

SPECIAL PLANTS

#	PLANTS	TYPE	LOCATION	WATERING FREQUENCY
1				
2				
3				
4				
5				
6				
7				
8				
9				
10				
11				

HOUSE PLANT *CARE LOG*

Date: / / /

PORCH PLANTS

KITCHENPLANTS

LIVING ROOM PLANTS

SPECIAL PLANTS

#	PLANTS	TYPE	LOCATION	WATERING FREQUENCY
1				
2				
3				
4				
5				
6				
7				
8				
9				
10				
11				

HOUSE PLANT *CARE LOG*

Date: / / /

PORCH PLANTS

KITCHENPLANTS

LIVING ROOM PLANTS

SPECIAL PLANTS

#	PLANTS	TYPE	LOCATION	WATERING FREQUENCY
1				
2				
3				
4				
5				
6				
7				
8				
9				
10				
11				

HOUSE PLANT *CARE LOG*

Date: / / /

PORCH PLANTS

KITCHENPLANTS

LIVING ROOM PLANTS

SPECIAL PLANTS

#	PLANTS	TYPE	LOCATION	WATERING FREQUENCY
1				
2				
3				
4				
5				
6				
7				
8				
9				
10				
11				

HOUSE PLANT *CARE LOG*

Date: / / /

PORCH PLANTS

KITCHENPLANTS

LIVING ROOM PLANTS

SPECIAL PLANTS

#	PLANTS	TYPE	LOCATION	WATERING FREQUENCY
1				
2				
3				
4				
5				
6				
7				
8				
9				
10				
11				

HOUSE PLANT *CARE LOG*

Date: / / /

PORCH PLANTS

KITCHENPLANTS

LIVING ROOM PLANTS

SPECIAL PLANTS

#	PLANTS	TYPE	LOCATION	WATERING FREQUENCY
1				
2				
3				
4				
5				
6				
7				
8				
9				
10				
11				

HOUSE PLANT *CARE LOG*   *Date: / / /*

PORCH PLANTS

KITCHENPLANTS

LIVING ROOM PLANTS

SPECIAL PLANTS

#	PLANTS	TYPE	LOCATION	WATERING FREQUENCY
1				
2				
3				
4				
5				
6				
7				
8				
9				
10				
11				

HOUSE PLANT *CARE LOG*

Date: / / /

PORCH PLANTS

KITCHENPLANTS

LIVING ROOM PLANTS

SPECIAL PLANTS

#	PLANTS	TYPE	LOCATION	WATERING FREQUENCY
1				
2				
3				
4				
5				
6				
7				
8				
9				
10				
11				

HOUSE PLANT *CARE LOG*   *Date: / / /*

PORCH PLANTS

KITCHENPLANTS

LIVING ROOM PLANTS

SPECIAL PLANTS

#	PLANTS	TYPE	LOCATION	WATERING FREQUENCY
1				
2				
3				
4				
5				
6				
7				
8				
9				
10				
11				

HOUSE PLANT *CARE LOG*

Date: / / /

PORCH PLANTS

KITCHENPLANTS

LIVING ROOM PLANTS

SPECIAL PLANTS

#	PLANTS	TYPE	LOCATION	WATERING FREQUENCY
1				
2				
3				
4				
5				
6				
7				
8				
9				
10				
11				

HOUSE PLANT *CARE LOG*

Date: / / /

PORCH PLANTS

KITCHENPLANTS

LIVING ROOM PLANTS

SPECIAL PLANTS

#	PLANTS	TYPE	LOCATION	WATERING FREQUENCY
1				
2				
3				
4				
5				
6				
7				
8				
9				
10				
11				

HOUSE PLANT *CARE LOG*

Date: / / /

PORCH PLANTS

KITCHENPLANTS

LIVING ROOM PLANTS

SPECIAL PLANTS

#	PLANTS	TYPE	LOCATION	WATERING FREQUENCY
1				
2				
3				
4				
5				
6				
7				
8				
9				
10				
11				

HOUSE PLANT *CARE LOG*

Date: / / /

PORCH PLANTS

KITCHENPLANTS

LIVING ROOM PLANTS

SPECIAL PLANTS

#	PLANTS	TYPE	LOCATION	WATERING FREQUENCY
1				
2				
3				
4				
5				
6				
7				
8				
9				
10				
11				

HOUSE PLANT *CARE LOG*   *Date:* / / /

PORCH PLANTS

KITCHENPLANTS

LIVING ROOM PLANTS

SPECIAL PLANTS

#	PLANTS	TYPE	LOCATION	WATERING FREQUENCY
1				
2				
3				
4				
5				
6				
7				
8				
9				
10				
11				

HOUSE PLANT *CARE LOG*   *Date: / / /*

PORCH PLANTS

KITCHENPLANTS

LIVING ROOM PLANTS

SPECIAL PLANTS

#	PLANTS	TYPE	LOCATION	WATERING FREQUENCY
1				
2				
3				
4				
5				
6				
7				
8				
9				
10				
11				

HOUSE PLANT *CARE LOG*

Date: / / /

PORCH PLANTS

KITCHENPLANTS

LIVING ROOM PLANTS

SPECIAL PLANTS

#	PLANTS	TYPE	LOCATION	WATERING FREQUENCY
1				
2				
3				
4				
5				
6				
7				
8				
9				
10				
11				

HOUSE PLANT *CARE LOG*   *Date: / / /*

PORCH PLANTS

KITCHENPLANTS

LIVING ROOM PLANTS

SPECIAL PLANTS

#	PLANTS	TYPE	LOCATION	WATERING FREQUENCY
1				
2				
3				
4				
5				
6				
7				
8				
9				
10				
11				

HOUSE PLANT *CARE LOG*

Date: / / /

PORCH PLANTS

KITCHENPLANTS

LIVING ROOM PLANTS

SPECIAL PLANTS

#	PLANTS	TYPE	LOCATION	WATERING FREQUENCY
1				
2				
3				
4				
5				
6				
7				
8				
9				
10				
11				

HOUSE PLANT *CARE LOG*

Date: / / /

PORCH PLANTS

KITCHENPLANTS

LIVING ROOM PLANTS

SPECIAL PLANTS

#	PLANTS	TYPE	LOCATION	WATERING FREQUENCY
1				
2				
3				
4				
5				
6				
7				
8				
9				
10				
11				

HOUSE PLANT *CARE LOG*

Date: / / /

PORCH PLANTS

KITCHENPLANTS

LIVING ROOM PLANTS

SPECIAL PLANTS

#	PLANTS	TYPE	LOCATION	WATERING FREQUENCY
1				
2				
3				
4				
5				
6				
7				
8				
9				
10				
11				

HOUSE PLANT *CARE LOG*   *Date: / / /*

PORCH PLANTS

KITCHENPLANTS

LIVING ROOM PLANTS

SPECIAL PLANTS

#	PLANTS	TYPE	LOCATION	WATERING FREQUENCY
1				
2				
3				
4				
5				
6				
7				
8				
9				
10				
11				

HOUSE PLANT *CARE LOG*   *Date: / / /*

PORCH PLANTS

KITCHENPLANTS

LIVING ROOM PLANTS

SPECIAL PLANTS

#	PLANTS	TYPE	LOCATION	WATERING FREQUENCY
1				
2				
3				
4				
5				
6				
7				
8				
9				
10				
11				

HOUSE PLANT *CARE LOG*

Date: / / /

PORCH PLANTS

KITCHENPLANTS

LIVING ROOM PLANTS

SPECIAL PLANTS

#	PLANTS	TYPE	LOCATION	WATERING FREQUENCY
1				
2				
3				
4				
5				
6				
7				
8				
9				
10				
11				

HOUSE PLANT *CARE LOG*

Date: / / /

PORCH PLANTS

KITCHENPLANTS

LIVING ROOM PLANTS

SPECIAL PLANTS

#	PLANTS	TYPE	LOCATION	WATERING FREQUENCY
1				
2				
3				
4				
5				
6				
7				
8				
9				
10				
11				

HOUSE PLANT *CARE LOG* *Date: / / /*

PORCH PLANTS

KITCHENPLANTS

LIVING ROOM PLANTS

SPECIAL PLANTS

#	PLANTS	TYPE	LOCATION	WATERING FREQUENCY
1				
2				
3				
4				
5				
6				
7				
8				
9				
10				
11				

HOUSE PLANT *CARE LOG*

Date: / / /

PORCH PLANTS

KITCHENPLANTS

LIVING ROOM PLANTS

SPECIAL PLANTS

#	PLANTS	TYPE	LOCATION	WATERING FREQUENCY
1				
2				
3				
4				
5				
6				
7				
8				
9				
10				
11				

HOUSE PLANT *CARE LOG*

Date: / / /

PORCH PLANTS

KITCHENPLANTS

LIVING ROOM PLANTS

SPECIAL PLANTS

#	PLANTS	TYPE	LOCATION	WATERING FREQUENCY
1				
2				
3				
4				
5				
6				
7				
8				
9				
10				
11				

HOUSE PLANT *CARE LOG*

Date: / / /

PORCH PLANTS

KITCHENPLANTS

LIVING ROOM PLANTS

SPECIAL PLANTS

#	PLANTS	TYPE	LOCATION	WATERING FREQUENCY
1				
2				
3				
4				
5				
6				
7				
8				
9				
10				
11				

HOUSE PLANT *CARE LOG*

Date: / / /

PORCH PLANTS

KITCHENPLANTS

LIVING ROOM PLANTS

SPECIAL PLANTS

#	PLANTS	TYPE	LOCATION	WATERING FREQUENCY
1				
2				
3				
4				
5				
6				
7				
8				
9				
10				
11				

HOUSE PLANT *CARE LOG*

Date: / / /

PORCH PLANTS

KITCHENPLANTS

LIVING ROOM PLANTS

SPECIAL PLANTS

#	PLANTS	TYPE	LOCATION	WATERING FREQUENCY
1				
2				
3				
4				
5				
6				
7				
8				
9				
10				
11				

HOUSE PLANT *CARE LOG*

Date: / / /

PORCH PLANTS

KITCHENPLANTS

LIVING ROOM PLANTS

SPECIAL PLANTS

#	PLANTS	TYPE	LOCATION	WATERING FREQUENCY
1				
2				
3				
4				
5				
6				
7				
8				
9				
10				
11				

HOUSE PLANT *CARE LOG*

Date: / / /

PORCH PLANTS

KITCHENPLANTS

LIVING ROOM PLANTS

SPECIAL PLANTS

#	PLANTS	TYPE	LOCATION	WATERING FREQUENCY
1				
2				
3				
4				
5				
6				
7				
8				
9				
10				
11				

HOUSE PLANT *CARE LOG*

Date: / / /

PORCH PLANTS

KITCHENPLANTS

LIVING ROOM PLANTS

SPECIAL PLANTS

#	PLANTS	TYPE	LOCATION	WATERING FREQUENCY
1				
2				
3				
4				
5				
6				
7				
8				
9				
10				
11				

HOUSE PLANT *CARE LOG*

Date: / / /

PORCH PLANTS

KITCHENPLANTS

LIVING ROOM PLANTS

SPECIAL PLANTS

#	PLANTS	TYPE	LOCATION	WATERING FREQUENCY
1				
2				
3				
4				
5				
6				
7				
8				
9				
10				
11				

HOUSE PLANT *CARE LOG*　　　　　　*Date:* / / /

PORCH PLANTS

KITCHENPLANTS

LIVING ROOM PLANTS

SPECIAL PLANTS

#	PLANTS	TYPE	LOCATION	WATERING FREQUENCY
1				
2				
3				
4				
5				
6				
7				
8				
9				
10				
11				

HOUSE PLANT *CARE LOG*   *Date: / / /*

PORCH PLANTS

KITCHENPLANTS

LIVING ROOM PLANTS

SPECIAL PLANTS

#	PLANTS	TYPE	LOCATION	WATERING FREQUENCY
1				
2				
3				
4				
5				
6				
7				
8				
9				
10				
11				

HOUSE PLANT *CARE LOG*   *Date: / / /*

PORCH PLANTS

KITCHENPLANTS

LIVING ROOM PLANTS

SPECIAL PLANTS

#	PLANTS	TYPE	LOCATION	WATERING FREQUENCY
1				
2				
3				
4				
5				
6				
7				
8				
9				
10				
11				

HOUSE PLANT *CARE LOG*

Date: / / /

PORCH PLANTS

KITCHENPLANTS

LIVING ROOM PLANTS

SPECIAL PLANTS

#	PLANTS	TYPE	LOCATION	WATERING FREQUENCY
1				
2				
3				
4				
5				
6				
7				
8				
9				
10				
11				

HOUSE PLANT *CARE LOG*

Date: **/ / /**

PORCH PLANTS

KITCHENPLANTS

LIVING ROOM PLANTS

SPECIAL PLANTS

#	PLANTS	TYPE	LOCATION	WATERING FREQUENCY
1				
2				
3				
4				
5				
6				
7				
8				
9				
10				
11				

HOUSE PLANT *CARE LOG*   *Date: / / /*

PORCH PLANTS

KITCHENPLANTS

LIVING ROOM PLANTS

SPECIAL PLANTS

#	PLANTS	TYPE	LOCATION	WATERING FREQUENCY
1				
2				
3				
4				
5				
6				
7				
8				
9				
10				
11				

HOUSE PLANT *CARE LOG*   *Date: / / /*

PORCH PLANTS

KITCHENPLANTS

LIVING ROOM PLANTS

SPECIAL PLANTS

#	PLANTS	TYPE	LOCATION	WATERING FREQUENCY
1				
2				
3				
4				
5				
6				
7				
8				
9				
10				
11				

HOUSE PLANT *CARE LOG*

Date: / / /

PORCH PLANTS

KITCHENPLANTS

LIVING ROOM PLANTS

SPECIAL PLANTS

#	PLANTS	TYPE	LOCATION	WATERING FREQUENCY
1				
2				
3				
4				
5				
6				
7				
8				
9				
10				
11				

HOUSE PLANT *CARE LOG*   *Date: / / /*

PORCH PLANTS

KITCHENPLANTS

LIVING ROOM PLANTS

SPECIAL PLANTS

#	PLANTS	TYPE	LOCATION	WATERING FREQUENCY
1				
2				
3				
4				
5				
6				
7				
8				
9				
10				
11				

HOUSE PLANT *CARE LOG*   *Date: / / /*

PORCH PLANTS

KITCHENPLANTS

LIVING ROOM PLANTS

SPECIAL PLANTS

#	PLANTS	TYPE	LOCATION	WATERING FREQUENCY
1				
2				
3				
4				
5				
6				
7				
8				
9				
10				
11				

HOUSE PLANT *CARE LOG*   *Date: / / /*

PORCH PLANTS

KITCHENPLANTS

LIVING ROOM PLANTS

SPECIAL PLANTS

#	PLANTS	TYPE	LOCATION	WATERING FREQUENCY
1				
2				
3				
4				
5				
6				
7				
8				
9				
10				
11				

HOUSE PLANT *CARE LOG*

Date: / / /

PORCH PLANTS

KITCHENPLANTS

LIVING ROOM PLANTS

SPECIAL PLANTS

#	PLANTS	TYPE	LOCATION	WATERING FREQUENCY
1				
2				
3				
4				
5				
6				
7				
8				
9				
10				
11				

HOUSE PLANT *CARE LOG*

Date: / / /

PORCH PLANTS

KITCHENPLANTS

LIVING ROOM PLANTS

SPECIAL PLANTS

#	PLANTS	TYPE	LOCATION	WATERING FREQUENCY
1				
2				
3				
4				
5				
6				
7				
8				
9				
10				
11				

HOUSE PLANT *CARE LOG*   *Date: / / /*

PORCH PLANTS

KITCHENPLANTS

LIVING ROOM PLANTS

SPECIAL PLANTS

#	PLANTS	TYPE	LOCATION	WATERING FREQUENCY
1				
2				
3				
4				
5				
6				
7				
8				
9				
10				
11				

HOUSE PLANT *CARE LOG*   *Date: / / /*

PORCH PLANTS

KITCHENPLANTS

LIVING ROOM PLANTS

SPECIAL PLANTS

#	PLANTS	TYPE	LOCATION	WATERING FREQUENCY
1				
2				
3				
4				
5				
6				
7				
8				
9				
10				
11				

HOUSE PLANT *CARE LOG*   *Date: / / /*

PORCH PLANTS

KITCHENPLANTS

LIVING ROOM PLANTS

SPECIAL PLANTS

#	PLANTS	TYPE	LOCATION	WATERING FREQUENCY
1				
2				
3				
4				
5				
6				
7				
8				
9				
10				
11				

Printed in Great Britain
by Amazon